Run with the Torch

1995-96 NWMS READING BOOKS

RESOURCE BOOK FOR THE LEADER

TOUCHING LIVES THROUGH SHARING
Edited by Beverlee Borbe

FOR THE READER

ARROWS OF THE ALMIGHTY
The Story of William Bromley,
Pioneer Missionary to Papua New Guinea
By A. A. E. Berg

FURLOUGHS, FURLONGS, AND POTLUCK DINNERS
Stories from the Deputation Trail
By A. Brent Cobb

MY LIFE AMONG THE NAVAJO
A Ministry to Body and Soul
By Beulah Campbell

RUN WITH THE TORCH
The Church of the Nazarene in El Salvador
By Eunice Bryant

BRINGING GOD'S WORD TO GUATEMALA
The Life and Work of William and Betty Sedat
By Lorraine O. Schultz

TREASURES IN THE DARKNESS
Stories from Behind Broken Walls
By Sharon R. Martin

Run
WITH
THE
TORCH

The Church of the Nazarene
in El Salvador

EUNICE BRYANT

Nazarene Publishing House
Kansas City, Mo.

Copyright 1995
by Nazarene Publishing House

ISBN 083-411-5328

Printed in the
United States of America

Cover Design: Crandall Vail and Michael Walsh

10   9   8   7   6   5   4   3   2   1

I dedicate
this small book to the memory of my mother,
Leone B. Kendall, who helped develop in my heart a
vigorous sense of mission, then backed Larry and me
with faithful intercession as we responded to the
divine call and served in Latin America.

Contents

EUNICE BRYANT served the Church of the Nazarene in missionary service for 29 years. She and her husband, Larry, have taught in the Bible college in Cobán, Guatemala, pioneered the work of the church in El Salvador, and served in Peru and at the former Spanish-American seminary in San Antonio, Texas. The Bryants make their home in Olathe, Kansas.

Preface

During our years of missionary ministry among the Guatemalans of Central America, we were keenly interested in the dramatic presentations of their historic traditions. One of these was their relay race with lighted torches on September 15, commemorating their independence from Spain, which occurred in 1821. We watched a team of eager runners who passed our home with lighted torches and were told that these participants would run to an appointed meeting place, where they would encounter other runners who would grab the torches and continue the relay.

What we saw was only a small segment of the big picture, for as these young men from our own locality were initiating their part of the race, others in various parts of Central America were lighting their torches and beginning their part of the relay. Those runners who were strongest and who reached the cities that were mapped out for them received honors, but some had not prepared themselves adequately for the race. These fell by the wayside, fainted, or became too weary or too sick to continue the race.

The participants met in principal cities, and the last group who received the lighted torches would run to the capital city of the adjoining nation, so that capital was united with capital. It was a picturesque celebration of the independence these nations now enjoyed and of the unity that existed among them.

As Larry and I have worked in Guatemala and El Salvador, this fascinating Olympic tradition has come to my mind many times. I have thought of our own ministry as being a part of an important relay team. The torch **we** carry is also a celebration of independence—independence from the slavery of sin. It dates clear back to Calvary, then personally to the day our own sins were forgiven, and later to that day when the Holy Spirit cleansed us in entire sanctification.

The flame of our torch represents the purity God has achieved in our hearts, but it is not a cleansing simply to be enjoyed by the recipient. Our light is to be shared. We are called to be energetic runners in a relay race that will not be complete until all participants meet around God's throne. We dare not faint or fall by the wayside.

As we run, enabled by the power of the Holy Spirit, we know that we are only a small segment of the great relay. Some day we will be passing our torch into the eager hands of those who will continue the race in our place when the Lord calls us home. In the meantime, may we be "blameless and harmless, children of God without fault in the midst of a crooked and perverse generation, among whom we shine as lights in the world, holding fast the word of life" (Phil. 2:15-16, author's paraphrase).

Acknowledgments

A missionary never has the luxury of declaring, "I did this all by myself!" Even recounting in a pocket-sized book the high points of a denomination's ministry in a given country is likely to represent the united efforts of several writers. This production is no exception.

I owe a debt of gratitude to Lilly de Jongh Osborne, author of *Four Keys to El Salvador,* a book rich in background material. Two issues of *World Mission* magazine (September 1992 and March 1994) have also been especially helpful in supplying data that treats the occurrences in El Salvador during those years when our ministry to Latin America took us elsewhere.

Members of my family who faithfully preserved my letters across the years provided a major source of detailed information. Some of my recall would have been fuzzy without this correspondence. Thanks to these thoughtful coworkers who did not condemn my letters to "File 13."

Bulletins provided by Tim Mastin and fresh updates from Dr. and Mrs. Frank Moore, Dr. Cecilia Meléndez, and Ramón and Julia Campos gave the book the contemporary perspective it needed.

Mr. Tim Crutcher of NWMS added valuable suggestions while the project was in the process. My sincere appreciation for your help, Tim!

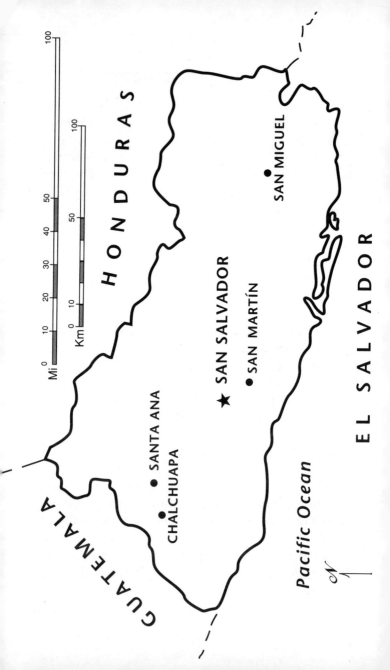

Introduction

El Salvador is one of the most densely populated countries in the world. It is the smallest among the sister republics of Central America, but its miniature size does not detract from its intrinsic value. It is a country of lush, semitropical vegetation, colorful birds and butterflies, lovely lakes, and volcanic mountains. For an artist who enjoys painting the beauties of nature or for a poet who prefers expressing his impressions with words, it is a veritable paradise.

El Salvador is also a favorite haunt for birdwatchers, shell collectors, and scientists who are interested in butterflies. Alberto Muyshondt, a Salvadoran specialist in the study of butterflies, has discovered that in his small country there are at least 350 distinctively different types of butterflies.

The Indian name Cuzcatlán (coos-cot-LAHN), a favorite name applied to El Salvador in its early history and still preferred among many of its citizens, means "the land of precious things." This name provides a highly appropriate description of the country itself, and if it were changed to "the land of precious *people*" it would be even more appropriate.

But the Spanish name, El Salvador (The Savior), has become the accepted name of the country, and San Salvador (Holy Savior) the name of the capital city. This is the precious name Christian missionaries lift up as they minister to the precious people who live in "the land of precious things."

As we entered this lovely Central American country, our first step was naturally that of bonding with the people. From day one we were delighted with the warmth of our new friends. The Salvadoran is very friendly and open and is not afraid to take the initiative in developing new friendships.

One of the most attractive features of these people, who even in 1964 were already on the brink of a serious civil war, is their ability to laugh in the midst of their problems. Often their missionaries chuckled with them as they poked fun at their situation or even at themselves—or at the North Americans!

Since theirs is the smallest Central American country, some of their wit is expressed in hyperboles concerning their size. One favorite story is that the only reason Hitler failed to bomb their republic during the Second World War was that on the day he announced his plan to destroy that country, his officers examined the map and could not find El Salvador because a fly had descended on the map and had landed on the very spot they were seeking!

This delightful characteristic was frequently expressed by the families who joined the Church of the Nazarene in El Salvador. The Murgas and the Navas, some of our first Salvadoran Nazarenes, are good examples. Neither family had a car, but with eyes brimming with mirth, they would tell us that they had had a difficult time making their decision

14

as to which car they would use for coming to Sunday School, the Mercury or the Lincoln! (The Navas lived a half block from the church.)

The Navas family had even taught their parrot to join in the fun. It would make sounds that imitated perfectly a person cleaning his teeth and rinsing his mouth. Since guests always laughed at this show, he would end the procedure with a raucous guffaw. After a few minutes, he would address the visitors saying, "Go home! Go home!" and would add another hearty "laugh."

The Salvadorans are just as sharp in their humor concerning the United States. One day when some of our believers were visiting us in our home, I mentioned that I had discovered some cockroaches in our house that day and that they were white. It was the first time in my life that I had ever seen a white cockroach. One of the ladies in the group quickly quipped that even the cockroaches of these North Americans were white.

Vitality, friendliness, graciousness, wit, good humor, creativity, and the ability to adjust to difficult situations were only a few of the positive qualities we observed as we became more intimately acquainted with the Salvadorans. They quickly won our hearts.

EL SALVADOR

General Information

Area: 8,260 square miles (21,476 square kilometers)—about the size of Massachusetts

Government: Republic

Population: 5.9 million (1995 approximation)

Density: 714 persons per square mile

Religions: 75% Roman Catholic, 20% Protestant, 5% other (Baha'is, Jehovah's Witnesses, Mormons, and nonreligious)

Language: Spanish

Literacy rate: 65%

Church of the Nazarene

Districts

El Salvador Central (regular district): District Superintendent Ramón Campos

El Salvador East (national mission district): District Superintendent Saúl Lucero

El Salvador West (national mission district): District Superintendent Guillermo Alfredo Perdomo

Members: 3,488

Churches: 32

Ordained elders: 11

Licensed ministers: 20

Missionaries: 0

FLAG: The Salvadoran flag has three bands. The top and bottom ones are a dark grayish blue. The middle band is white, with an emblem.

The Valley of Hammocks

CUZCATLÁN AND EL SALVADOR are not the only significant names that have been applied to this beautiful country. The area where the capital city is now located has been problematic since historic times, chiefly because of its volcanic threats and earthquakes. Due to the frequent movement of the earth, it has earned for itself the unenviable name of "The Valley of Hammocks." The destructive earthquake that occurred in 1965 gives substance to this descriptive title.

* * *

It is May 1965. There have been 9,000 earth tremors during the last three months, and now there has been an earthquake measuring over seven on the Richter scale. The possibility of death beneath weighty beams and collapsed walls sends terror-stricken family members wading through the debris, hoping against hope that sons, daughters, or parents might still have a chance.

"Did you hear that soft cry?" a young mother asks her husband. Marta digs anxiously as her heart beats with fresh hope. She turns to Ronaldo, who shakes his head and tries to remind her that after all these hours of searching, their baby couldn't possibly be alive. He would like to encourage her, but he feels he must be realistic. Death and devastation surround them on all sides.

A few minutes before, Marta and Ronaldo had stopped their fruitless search long enough to watch as soldiers uncovered a few still bodies—a father who obviously had thrown himself across his wife to protect her and a tiny infant under both of them, whom the mother had tried to save.

My husband, Larry, was present when those three inert members of one family were unearthed. He was also present when the military men pulled a woman from the rubble and laid her on a truck bed along with many others who had been taken from the debris. But unlike the rest on that stack of bodies, the woman suddenly sat up, looked around, and hastily jumped from the truck and ran away. The huge crowd of observers clapped and cheered as she disappeared. But Marta and Ronaldo kept on searching, as did many others like them.

As fellow searchers and observers moved about with strained expressions, some with tears, Larry was reminded that a few hours ago those people stacked on the truck bed were very much alive, full of hope and of redemptive possibilities. The awful reality of limited opportunities gripped his soul.

But not everyone was empathetic with those who were in grief. The hours passed, and thieves began their follow-up, sorting through the destruction to recover any possible treasures that might remain for those families who had lost everything.

An elderly lady had wrapped herself in a thin blanket, along with her few remaining possessions that had survived the earthquake. She was totally exhausted after a day of searching for friends who had disappeared. Suddenly she sensed that she was being carried away. She shrieked in horror, and the startled "treasure seekers" dropped her and fled in terror, afraid of the military police who might be in the area, protecting the people who, in turn, were guarding their scanty leftovers.

* * *

This is El Salvador, where my husband and I ministered for 12 years. Since 1964, when we entered this fascinating country as pioneer missionaries for the Church of the Nazarene, El Salvador has suffered thousands of earth tremors, two major earthquakes, 10 long years of civil war, and a short period of serious hostilities with Honduras, a next-door neighbor. In the civil war, at least 70,000 people lost their lives, and thousands more were forced to emigrate to other countries.

Obviously, missionaries who would dedicate themselves to serving this land of precious things and precious people would need to adapt to the unpleasant realities of constantly suffering fellow humans, who would need more than a Band-Aid gospel. While Salvadorans tread on shaky terrain and experience material losses and the sudden death of members of their families, they need the unshakable certainties of a gospel that is based on the eternal truths of God's Word.

As we listened intently to people from various economic positions and from diverse political ideologies, we became increasingly aware of our ministerial priorities. We came to the conclusion that our major task would be that of teaching, preaching, and living scriptural holiness in a country that had experienced limited exposure to this doctrine.

2

Pioneer Nazarene Torchbearers

BEFORE ANY GUATEMALAN or North American missionaries had planted the flag of the Church of the Nazarene in Salvadoran territory, Dr. H. T. Reza, a gifted Mexican preacher, had been broadcasting weekly messages on "La Hora Nazarena" (The Nazarene Hour). Many of his sermons were clear-cut holiness messages. These made an impact on listeners and opened the way for Nazarenes who later would evangelize and plant churches in many parts of Latin America. El Salvador was one of the countries that received this advantage.

Israel Bolaños (boh-LAHN-yoce), a bright young Salvadoran who had graduated from the Spanish-American Nazarene Seminary in San Antonio, longed to see our church established in his own country. By 1957, the burden had become heavy enough on his heart that he went to Guatemala City and talked it over with Pastor Federico Guillermo: "If you'll back me up and help me establish a church in my own country, I'll pastor the church and support myself by working in our International Airport. I won't expect the Church of the Nazarene to support me financially. Just give me a place to work and a few fellow Nazarenes to help me make a successful initial impact."

In response to Israel's plea, a number of people joined with this young Salvadoran to hold special meetings and open a Nazarene mission in San Martín, a small town near San Salvador, the capital city. These included Rev. Federico Guillermo, Rev. Joel Buenafé, Robert Ingram, Larry Bryant, Ernestina López and Amparo Ruano (two very active members of First Church in Guatemala City), and the men's quartet from our Bible institute in Cobán, Guatemala.

This team stayed only a few days, but their ministry was blessed of the Lord. The Bible school quartet was as excellent as a professional group, and Federico Guillermo and Joel Buenafé were both very capable preachers. As a consequence of the ministry of this group of Guatemalan and North American missionaries, 16 persons were won to the Lord, and Israel eagerly undertook the task of nourishing these new converts.

Israel Bolaños was highly talented as a public speaker and had a beautiful tenor voice for singing. God had given him a natural eloquence and dramatic ability that gave him unusual advantages. Unfortunately, his schedule at the Salvadoran international airport conflicted with his pastoral duties, so the new work did not thrive. Finally, the new mission was closed. By the time Larry and I arrived in El Salvador, Israel was struggling with a sense of failure and needed encouragement.

Israel was one of the first Salvadorans who knocked at the door of the rented trailer where we spent our first few weeks after arriving in his country. He sat in our living room and confessed his spiritual needs and expressed his desire to get back into full-time Christian work. He told us: "I am still employed at the airport and have a responsible position. I am not complaining about that job, but I feel the Lord has called me to a more important task. I can't avoid His call to ministry. It burns in my heart. Life has become empty and meaningless to me. As I look at the statistics for my country, I realize that in all probability I have only a few more years to live, and of what do those years consist?— a dull, repetitious cycle of eating, working, and sleeping and eating, working, and sleeping."

Israel was suffering from a sense of guilt and from depression. We prayed with him and encouraged him to walk in all the new light the Lord was shedding on his heart. But we knew when he left our home that day that he still had deep needs.

When we initiated a Nazarene mission in a residential part of the capital city, Israel was one of our most faithful helpers, but he was still seeking earnestly for an experience of entire sanctification. However, he used his opportunities for Christian service during that prolonged period of spiritual search. He sang solos in the services, preached occasional messages, and helped us pray with seekers at the altar. His ministry around the altar was espe-

cially valuable, since there were so few fellow believers who had experience in altar work.

Another special contribution Israel provided
was that of giving these missionaries insights into
the culture of his country. Our previous 12 years of
experience in Guatemala applied significantly in
many areas of our ministry, but we had much to
learn. El Salvador was different. Even parts of her
vocabulary were different. Furthermore, we were
now working in a capital city as church planters
rather than as faculty members of a Bible college in
a much quieter mountain town. We needed the expertise of a man like Israel.

Among other new discoveries was the fact that
the Salvadoran, in general, wants to please his
friends and feels obligated to make a person feel
happy when he or she makes a request. This does
not necessarily mean that he will feel obligated to
fulfill his promise. His dedication to courtesy at the
moment dictates his response. We learned this lesson the hard way while doing visitation evange-
lism. We received promises from people to be in the
church services the following Sunday and assur-
ances that they were "enchanted" by our visit, but
this was to no avail. Actually, if everyone who
promised to come *had* come, there would not be
space for them!

The day finally arrived when Israel made a full
surrender to the Lord and gave a clear testimony
that the Lord had sanctified him. The joy of the
Lord literally radiated from his expressive eyes. His
testimony and changed life were a blessing to his

missionaries and the new converts and a challenge to the unsaved. But before long, he began to feel a strong urge to move to the United States. Naturally, we, along with his other friends, tried to discourage this move, but he seemed to feel that this was best for him and his family. It was with sad hearts that we watched him go.

Among the pioneers mentioned at the beginning of this chapter were two energetic, hardworking Guatemalan ladies, members of First Church in Guatemala City. Their story of involvement in the work of the Church of the Nazarene in El Salvador is quite different from the Bolaños story. They were part of the original scouting team that had surveyed the possibilities of our entering El Salvador and were involved in the initial victories at the San Martín mission.

When Rev. Federico Guillermo, by this time district superintendent of Guatemala, learned that North American missionaries were scheduled to open the work in August, he invited Ernestina López and Amparo Ruano to go to El Salvador and open Nazarene work there before we would arrive. Those two workers accepted the challenge. Of course, there was a certain amount of wholesome competition involved in this plan. Federico wanted Guatemala to enjoy the credit for having arrived first. Why not?

On May 17, 1964, Miss López and her helper, Miss Ruano, opened our first mission. They had chosen a very needy area of the capital for concentrating their efforts and had prepared the way with an intensive visitation program. Time has shown that their choice was in accord with God's will. These Guatemalan team members carried the torch into the darkness of intense spiritual, physical, and economic need. Ernestina and Amparo took many risks, ministering in what we would call an inner-city mission. They worked diligently at their task, so that by the time we arrived in August, that new mission had more than 80 people attending Sunday School.

Amparo and Ernestina had no car or church van in which to carry their new converts to Sunday School, but many times they would go early to a home and offer their services to the parents. They would dress the children and walk with them to the mission. Ernestina was a capable disciplinarian and was an expert in handling large groups of children.

When the earthquake occurred in 1965, these two workers helped distribute the beans, rice, and powdered milk that were made available by a $1,000 offering on the part of a Nazarene in the United States. Fifteen Nazarene families from First Mission had lost their homes, but Ernestina and Amparo did not limit their compassionate ministry to their own people. Catholics and Protestants were treated with equal Christian love. Once a week, for several weeks after the earthquake, these women would meet with people who had been left destitute by the earthquake and would provide them with basic foods.

First Mission was always hot and uncomfortable, but those two ladies were on the job night after night, teaching, preaching, exhorting, praying with seekers, and carrying a burden for the unsaved. A handsome young mechanic named Rafael Flores was one of the first converts in our First Mission, and "Cupid" began to play his special role. Amparo was quiet, reserved, and attractive, so attractive that little by little First Mission acquired a third helper. Not too long after First Mission had graduated into the category of First Church, Rafael and Amparo became husband and wife.

Among those first believers there were some who thought it would be wonderful to enter the ministry. They presumed they would have fewer temptations if they became Nazarene preachers! But Rafael did not choose the ministry to avoid temptations. His working with Ernestina and Amparo had exposed him to the harsh realities of pastoral experiences. His reason for taking his young wife to Costa Rica, where he studied for the ministry in our Nazarene seminary, was based on a definite divine call.

As pastors from Guatemala became available to help in El Salvador, Ernestina López was whisked off to Guatemala City. Leaders there had discovered her worth as a church planter. She had planted and nurtured, and God had given the increase. Now she was permitted to return to the much cooler climate of the neighboring capital city, where she employed the expertise she had gained from her ministry in San Salvador.

Rafael, Amparo, and little Elioenaí (ail-ee-oh-en-ah-EE) moved to a tiny student house on campus in Costa Rica. But that house had room for three more Flores children who were born during their parents' years of study. One can imagine the confusion of crying babies, feeding schedules, term papers, and tough exams: "Please, Amparo, do what you can to quiet Elioenaí. The library is closed for the night. It's pouring down rain. I'm stuck right here, and that boy is driving me up the wall. I have two final exams tomorrow, and I have read only half of the main textbook for the course on the theology of John Wesley."

And his patient little wife would do her best to quiet Elioenaí while she fed Bessie, Melquisedec, and Otoniel. But the Lord was preparing them for more demanding situations when they would assume the responsibilities of pastoring our Vista Hermosa Church in San Salvador.

When the Flores family returned from seminary and initiated their pastorate in Vista Hermosa, it appeared that they would have a cooperative and united group of believers in their church. But by that time, some of our churches were suffering from the political grasp for power that can creep into a church no matter where in the world it is.

A group of seemingly righteous men had wormed their way into positions of power in the local church and even at the district level. Only little by little did their evil intentions come to light. Apparently these men wanted to destroy our churches and initiate a substitute religious group that would be totally under their domination. Some even accused them of trying to steal Nazarene church properties for their own purposes.

Rafael and Amparo Flores and family

Rafael and Amparo suffered in silence as they watched the crowds diminish in the Sunday services and as they received less and less in the offering plates. They stretched their limited income to feed their growing children, but the pastor and his wife were going hungry. They determined to trust God and not mention their financial problems to the missionaries. They were sure God would do a miracle and provide for their needs. God definitely was not asleep, even though we missionaries had temporarily been unaware of the problem. Finally, we noticed the pale faces and undernourished bodies of the Flores family and began to ask some straightforward questions.

"What's happened?" we asked. "You and your whole family look sick. What can we do to help you?" With reluctance, Rafael and Amparo explained that some men in their church had advised other members to quit tithing. They had told them that the Flores family claimed that they lived by faith and that God would provide for their needs. Their excuse was, "They say they live by faith. Let's quit tithing and see if God will take care of them!" Of course, God *did* take care of them, so well in fact that the troublemakers left the Vista Hermosa Church and joined another denomination. The Flores family kept running with the torch!

Guatemalan leaders of the Church of the Nazarene had already taken Ernestina López back and had given her a full schedule in her own country. Rafael Flores and his wife and children had served faithfully in Vista Hermosa and in our Jardín Church (which began as Second Mission) in San Salvador when they, too, received an invitation to pastor in Guatemala. Rafael was the first Salvadoran Nazarene to pastor in Guatemala.

But hardships followed the Flores family even after they had settled into their new ministry in Guatemala. One of these has kept them linked with fellow Nazarenes in the United States in a special relationship. Their little son Melquisedec lost an eye when a large firecracker exploded in his face. On various occasions, Melqui (as his family calls him) has confronted the need for delicate operations on the hole that was left in that portion of his face, and fellow Nazarenes have generously lent financial help to improve his appearance through these operations.

As a teenager, Melqui has bravely kept running as a Christian and as a student. He has shown a wholesome attitude in the midst of his problems and has sensed a divine call to serve as a missionary. So the torch is passed from country to country and from generation to generation.

3

Enthusiastic Beginners in the Race

A S WE PRAYED AND SOUGHT divine guidance for the initiation of a second Nazarene mission in the capital city, we were challenged by a friendly fellow Christian from a sister denomination. He told Larry that no evangelical group had ever established a mission in any residential area of the capital, and he felt it might be the Lord's will for the Nazarenes to take this brave step. Not far from the spot where our present Jardín Church of the Nazarene is now located, Larry and his friend stood and prayed about this challenging possibility. The more we sought the divine will on this question, the more certain we were that this was God's plan.

We had been cooperating with Ernestina and Amparo in First Mission during our first four months in El Salvador, but by January 1965 we were ready to hold our first service in Second Mission. We rented two rooms in a brand-new house that was located in a strategic spot for attracting young people. Actually, those rooms had been designed by the owner for a small bar and liquor store—a far cry from their more sacred use as the birthplace of what would eventually become Jardín Church of the Nazarene.

Despite a heavy program of house-to-house visitation to prepare the way, only 13 brave persons came on the Sunday the mission was opened. These ventured timidly into the rented rooms. They were frightened and showed it in their actions. Obviously, they were afraid of the crowds that had gathered outside. Three of those who had entered hurried out even before Sunday School classes had started.

On the first Sunday night 16 took the risk of entering the mission while a big crowd milled around outside. There seemed to be an electric current of fear that surrounded the house. When Larry encouraged them to enter, several hurried away, but our lovely daughter, Joyce, and our attractive Salvadoran assistant, Rosa Cristales, were more successful. (Needless to say, the greater part of the crowd that accepted the girls' invitation consisted of handsome young men!)

When these people hurried out the door at the close of the service, one of them turned to us and said, "Encantado! Encantado!" ("Enchanted! Enchanted!") I am not absolutely sure who might have enchanted him, but to their credit it should be mentioned that those who ventured inside gave excellent attention, despite the atmosphere of curiosity, fear, and suspicion that surrounded the building.

Larry went over to the mission the following day to sand some of the benches and apparently was able to do more teaching than the ordinary pastor accomplishes during two or three sermons. A group of young men came into the mission and really plied him with serious questions about Nazarene beliefs. They were interested in knowing what Nazarenes believe about the Virgin Mary. Do Nazarenes believe that Mary was born without inbred sin? Do Nazarenes use her as a medium of intercession in their prayers? Do Nazarenes call her "the Mother of God"? The young men seemed pleased that our church holds Mary in high regard, even though we do not accept several of the standard Roman Catholic beliefs about her. They had been told that evangelicals actually belittled the Virgin. Larry was able to remove this and several other doubts and unfounded prejudices that day.

We inaugurated a series of evangelistic services and discipled those who gave evidence of having made a definite decision for Christ. Many nights we would remain until late hours answering questions about Nazarene doctrines and rules of conduct. The young people who attended the services were curious to know what Nazarenes believe and why.

Some of the university students showed keen interest in the Nazarenes' attitude toward Marxism, but their discussions with us were more academic than religious. In fact, they showed more interest in their own political position than in the stance of the Church of the Nazarene on the question of the existence of God. As is true in every country in the world, El Salvador had been invaded by false teachers who had endeavored to tear away the moorings of the Christian faith.

Other obstacles faced by those new people who came to our church were much more practical than philosophical. In one of our discipling classes, the new believers tackled Nazarene concepts about dancing and movies. "What's wrong with going to movies?" they asked. "Why don't you believe in attending them? Some of them are quite decent." The teacher suggested that class members study newspaper advertisements for the movies during the week and that they bring examples to class the following week so that the entire group could discuss their content.

Interestingly enough, this study accomplished a great deal more than anything the teacher had to add! Some of the parents expressed their appreciation. Their teenagers' personal discoveries had made a difference in their set of values. One of the parents who expressed his gratitude later confessed that, before he had become a Nazarene, he had on various occasions sat in a theater during a movie and thought, "I surely hope Jesus will not come back while I'm here!"

Several of those who attended our Second Mission had a serious problem with alcohol. One of the problems with alcoholics was that they often were quite sincere in longing to overcome their alcoholism but were less interested in forsaking their other vices. It seemed difficult for them to realize that God calls for a total surrender. They wanted to bargain with the Lord.

However, in other cases there were more permanent results of our ministry to men who had this problem. A barber who lived near one of our missions had such a serious problem with drinking and "womanizing" that his wife had temporarily lost her mind and was in a psychiatric ward at the hospital. But the Lord convicted him, and he was beautifully saved and delivered from his vices. As a consequence of his salvation, his wife also was saved and was healed of her mental handicap. Because of the power of divine grace, she was enabled to adopt a precious little girl who was a result of her husband's previous meanderings, and that family became a part of the Church of the Nazarene.

It isn't possible to follow the entire story of many of our early Salvadoran Nazarenes, since several of them emigrated to other countries. During the civil war, every family was confronted with the decision of taking the risk of remaining or taking the risk of trying to carve out a new life in a different culture. Some have begun to return, but others have made such a firm adjustment in other countries that it is highly unlikely they will ever return to El Salvador for more than short visits with their relatives and friends.

Not everyone left, however, and those who stayed were enabled to run victoriously despite their circumstances. Roberto Reyes (RAY-yace) was one of those enthusiastic young Christians who joined the Church of the Nazarene during the beginning months of our work in Second Mission. He and several of his brothers and sisters attended with their father, who was a retired army colonel.

Roberto and other members of his family took part in discipling classes, special Bible studies, youth camps, Bible quizzing, and in almost every activity provided by the church. Some of his brothers and sisters were in and out of the church, but Roberto and Heriberto, the colonel, took their membership seriously.

Roberto had gone to the altar and had professed to be saved. He eagerly entered the discipling classes and began to prepare for baptism and for membership in the church. When his schedule as a student in the university conflicted with the discipling classes, he came to our home and earnestly sought for new light. As the small book being studied revealed areas that were new to him, Roberto wanted to know more.

"What do you mean by repentance?" he asked. "Do you mean that in order to be saved a person needs to repent and forsake *all* his sins?" "Yes," we answered. "It means to make a 180-degree turn in your journey. You quit doing those things you recognize as contrary to the will of God. Repentance is more than feeling sorry for your sins or simply quitting a few of them. True repentance requires an all-out forsaking of the sins you have been committing."

A quizzical expression clouded his face as the light began to penetrate. "Señora, I don't have the kind of experience we have been talking about. I see that I have never really repented of all my sins." There was disappointment in his voice, but I assured him that right there in the living room of our home God could come and help him make that kind of surrender. The chair where he had been seated became his altar, and the Lord graciously answered that sinner's prayer. He helped Roberto to repent and believe, and He saved him that day.

Roberto continued his medical studies in the university. It was a period when Marxism was highly in vogue among university students in that part of the world, and Roberto was subjected to the constant peer pressure of fellow students who had accepted atheism. Not only had they identified with it, but they insisted that others in their community take atheism seriously.

Despite this pressure, Roberto joined the Nazarene Bible quizzers and spent Sunday afternoons with young fellow Christians who were preparing for a national tournament and later an international competition. He was a keen quizzer and had the advantage of being able to memorize quite rapidly. Seemingly it was right during his study of the Epistle to the Hebrews that he suffered the strongest pressure from fellow students to forsake his Christian faith and join the crowd of rejecters. He seemed to wobble for a while, but the Lord helped him become "more than a conqueror."

Today, Roberto is still an active member of the Jardín Church of the Nazarene and a successful medical doctor. In addition to keeping up his own practice, he has made a substantial contribution to Compassionate Ministries. He and his wife, Connie, have a promising family. His two boys, Roberto, Jr., and David Ernesto, are involved in youth activities in the church.

David Ernesto was born with a very serious birth defect in his legs, but he refuses to be confined to a wheelchair. In fact, his story is dramatic enough to warrant its being published by itself. He has developed his arms and shoulders to the extent that he can manipulate them and navigate himself up and down stairs and out into the yard to play with the neighbors. He is a good student at school, and one of the school ball teams has elected him as their mascot. He has learned to play the organ and seems bent on making his life as meaningful as possible. In our Jardín Church, he sits quietly in his wheelchair, but the lively expression on his face as he participates in worship shows that he is really "running"!

Roberto's father, Colonel Heriberto Reyes, has stayed true to the Lord across the years and under pressure has shown a Christian spirit. When his parents died and it was time to divide the family properties among the heirs, the colonel, like Abraham, let others choose first. He had every right to select the best for himself, especially on the basis of his having an unusually large family to support, but he showed a Christlike spirit. He accepted what was left after others had chosen.

A much greater test came to the Reyes family during the civil war. One of Roberto's brothers decided to follow in his father's footsteps and join the military forces. He was a promising young man and anticipated a successful career in the army, but shortly after beginning this new chapter in his life, he was killed by a leftist guerrilla. Naturally, the whole family has struggled with severe temptations to hold resentments and feel bitterness toward the murderer.

Fellow Christians who have never experienced civil war and death at their own front door should take seriously the ministry of intercession for families like the Reyes family. At the same time, they should be encouraged by the persistence of these fellow runners who have suffered scars in the battle but keep on running for Christ.

4

On to Perfection

WELL, CELIA, WHAT DO YOU THINK of the Church of the Nazarene after our having visited their First Mission tonight?"

"I'd like to visit their Second Mission, which is much closer to our home. Really, Miguel, this would be a big change for us. We have belonged to one of the largest evangelical congregations here in the capital city for so many years, and to join a brand-new denomination would require some difficult adjustments."

"You're right. We'd have to take quite a bit of criticism from family and friends. What did you think of the idea mentioned by Mr. Bryant when we greeted him after the service tonight? When I told him we were thinking of leaving our own denomination and joining the Church of the Nazarene, he said he would need to talk to our pastor about our plans."

"That surprised me, but really he couldn't do otherwise without leaving the impression that he is a sheep robber. There surely are plenty of those in town."

Miguel and Celia Mejía (meh-HEE-ah), along with their four children, were not making their first contact with the Church of the Nazarene that hot evening when they visited our First Mission in San Salvador. They had listened various times to the radio messages preached by Dr. H. T. Reza on "La Hora Nazarena," and they had been impressed especially by his emphasis on the doctrine of holiness. Also, they were personal friends to Israel Bolaños.

However, there was an incomparably greater influence at work in their lives. They had been taught across the years that as long as they lived in the flesh they would continue to commit sins. Sanctification would be possible only in the hour of death. Also, they had heard innumerable times that they could never fall from grace. But little by little, the Holy Spirit had been dealing with them and convincing them that Christ's death on the Cross meant total victory over sin. God had not made that provision with the objective of producing sinning Christians.

Perhaps the first awakening that Miguel Mejía experienced regarding the theology of his church had come during a conference in which he was housed with a group of preachers. He was quite young but listened with keen interest to the conversation among pastors that was going on in an adjacent bedroom.

He heard one of those preachers, in whom he had a great deal of confidence, comment that their doctrine of perseverance (once in grace, always in grace) was essentially a dangerous doctrine. Miguel naturally perked up his ears and eavesdropped to catch the response of the group. He was surprised with the agreement others expressed but had to admit to himself that such a doctrine indeed opened the door to willful sinning and to a life of pretense. Miguel sensed a longing for real deliverance from sin—from willful sin and from inbred sin.

Now the years had passed since that flash of spiritual insight that occurred that night in his teens, and the Holy Spirit had faithfully tugged at his heart. Dr. Reza's messages, Israel Bolaños' personal testimony, and a gradually deepening hunger and thirst for Christian perfection combined to make Miguel a ripe candidate for entire sanctification.

We told the Mejías to pray about their decision to join the Church of the Nazarene. We said that we would join with them in this prayer but that we felt they should take time to be sure about this important step. They should find God's will and then act.

All of us took this assignment seriously. Miguel and Celia and their children prayed and sought the divine will concerning this question. While they were weighing the matter, the parents visited Second Mission only occasionally, but the four children came frequently and took part in activities of the Church of the Nazarene.

Perhaps six months had passed when one Sunday morning the entire Mejía family came to Second Mission and worshiped joyfully with the small group of new believers. At the close of the service,

Miguel cornered us and announced with certainty, "We have prayed earnestly and believe we have found the divine will for our family. We want to join the Church of the Nazarene. We are coming to you as hungry sheep, and we want to be fed!" And when he said "hungry," he really meant hungry! What a spiritual appetite Miguel and Celia evidenced as they sought for understanding of the doctrine of holiness and for the experience of entire sanctification!

They asked us to dedicate one evening per week to giving them special classes on this doctrine. They volunteered to come to our home rather than expecting us to visit their home or give the classes in the church. Several successive Monday evenings Miguel came straight from his work at Cidema, a company that sold farm equipment and other machinery. He came without supper and stayed till late hours, seeking earnestly for the truth. His wife came too, and the two of them thought through what H. Orton Wiley and W. T. Purkiser had written concerning the doctrine of holiness.

One of those Monday evenings, Miguel challenged us: "Let's close the theology textbooks and simply depend on what the Word of God has to teach us." And the more they delved into the Word, the hungrier they became for the type of perfection that they had begun to realize was obtainable in this life. Finally, with the help of the Holy Spirit, their faith took hold, and they were entirely sanctified. "Blessed are those who hunger and thirst for righteousness, for they will be filled" (Matt. 5:6).

In one sense, the long quest was over, but in another it had just begun. The Mejías had made a complete consecration to the Lord, and this included a great unknown bundle of future situations that God would reveal to them according to His own calendar. Their "eternal yes" would be tested over and over again.

Omar Mejía, their oldest son, watched his parents with interest and came to the conclusion that he, too, wanted to be sanctified. He could see the differences in their lives, and the Spirit deepened the spiritual hunger in his heart. He determined to read straight through the New Testament and discover for himself what the Lord had to say about a totally purified heart.

One evening Omar took two of his close teenage friends with him. They climbed a mountain, sat together, and read the New Testament, searching for truth concerning entire sanctification. A person can imagine the conversation that went on that night among those three earnest seekers: "Do you think people our age can live a sanctified life? We have such strong temptations to break over the prescribed limits and experiment with what is forbidden. Maybe sanctification is only for adults who are married and settled down with families."

Omar would have pointed out that he had observed youth in his church who gave every indication of having been really sanctified: "I believe these are just as purified and wholly sanctified as my parents are. And believe me, my parents have the real thing! And besides, the Bible doesn't put any age limits on this experience."

The boys studied and thought and prayed and compared insights. Finally, Omar suggested that they leave their mountain retreat and go to the Bryant home for further help. Long before daylight, the three appeared on our doorstep and explained their need for help. The Lord saw their sincerity and strengthened their faith, so that right there in our living room those three young men were sanctified.

The Mejías were a welcome addition to our Second Mission. Their home was a place where both rich and poor were received with equal warmth. "My home is your home" was not a mere truism. Mrs. Mejía was a gracious hostess, and the whole family knew how to make visitors feel welcome. Their continuous hospitality added a richness to the atmosphere of our new mission.

But graciousness was not their only contribution. Their home was a model of meaningful discipline. The family was conscious of the importance of controlling their time and investing it wisely. Omar was practicing on the piano eight hours per day and was looking forward to the time when he would become a world-famous pianist. (This fervor for long hours of practice almost cost him his life a few years later when he was studying in Europe. An angry neighbor shot through the window while Omar was practicing, and the young artist wisely decided to move to an area where his neighbors' homes would be farther separated from his studio!)

The Mejía family, *from left:* Miguel, Celia, Omar *(at piano)*, Enid, and Miguel, Jr.

Family discipline was such that when their television set broke down, the parents decided that they would not invest in getting it repaired, since it was robbing valuable time from more important matters, such as academic preparation. Celia was a teacher, and Miguel loved the classics in poetry and music. It is not surprising that Omar eventually became a world-famous pianist and that his sister, Aracely (ah-rah-CELL-ee), became a scholarly writer, spending 10 years in research to write a book about the earliest history of her country. And all four of the young Mejías were top-quality quizzers in the Bible quiz program, which was inaugurated in our Salvadoran Nazarene churches a few years after the Mejías had joined Second Mission.

The Mejías' dedication to study was quite evident in the Sunday School classes Miguel and Celia taught. Miguel once confessed in private that he never taught a Sunday School lesson without having spent at least three hours in preparation. And that preparation paid off in their spiritual influence on members of their classes. The Mejías had come announcing that they were hungry and wanted to be fed, and now they had become dedicated students of the Word who were equipped to feed others.

But beyond this type of dedication, this family early revealed their generosity. They were double tithers even before they became Nazarenes. In fact, when we learned this fact, we recognized more than ever the necessity of exercising caution in encouraging them to become members of our church. That could easily have been judged as mercenary, especially since our church was so new in their country and was economically limited.

Their double tithe was not the limit of their generosity. When funds had arrived for purchasing the lot for our Jardín Church but no funds were available for beginning the construction, the Mejías offered to mortgage their own home in order to facilitate matters while the church was waiting for Alabaster funds. And soon after the Jardín Church building was constructed, the Mejías purchased a brand-new grand piano for the church. Both Miguel and Omar played this piano for the church services.

Their generosity was contagious. Once, during a general church meeting at our Jardín Church, the members were making pledges for tiles for the church floor. At that point in the construction, there was only earth for a floor in the church. As people were pledging the number of tiles for which they would be responsible, Miguel pledged a sizable number for his wife and called her his mother. That set the atmosphere for hilarious giving. Others caught the humor of Miguel's pledge and began to pledge for other members of their own family, assigning them special fictitious relationships. But the pledges were made in earnest.

A brand-new discovery in the Mejías' consecration occurred in September 1972, during a session of the Advisory Board of our Nazarene Seminary of the Americas (now Nazarene University) in Costa Rica. Miguel had been chosen as El Salvador's lay representative to that board and had accompanied my husband, his district superintendent, to that meeting.

Rev. Howard Conrad, who was at that time the rector of the seminary, told the board members that he needed a business administrator for the school, and Larry received a sudden inspiration. He grabbed an index card from his pocket and wrote: "Miguel, business administrator; Celia, professor; Omar, music teacher," and he probably included the other three Mejía children with appropriate professional titles, despite their youth and inexperience.

He quietly handed the card to Miguel. One can only imagine the impact of that moment as Miguel read the note. He later confessed that his first reaction was negative. An unpleasant lump must have formed in his throat as he quickly reviewed the many adjustments he and his family had made in order to fit into that small, struggling new mission. They had left one of the most flourishing churches in their city to join in the demanding task of planting a new church for a different denomination. They had been ruthlessly criticized by some of their best friends, and now this missionary friend, in whom they had placed a great deal of confidence, was suggesting another radical step of faith.

Even though he was struggling with resentment toward what seemed to be an unfair proposition, he whispered to Larry, "We'll pray about it." As the whole Mejía family had joined in prayer concerning their becoming members of the Church of the Nazarene, now they united in earnest prayer asking for divine direction about this possible assignment. Of course, they were not alone in those prayers. Missionaries in El Salvador and in Costa Rica were concerned that they would accept this challenge only if, in fact, this were God's will.

Such a decision involved Miguel's leaving an income equivalent to $2,400 per month to accept around a tenth of this amount in Costa Rica. His income in El Salvador at that time was considered very good, and he had worked hard to achieve his financial status. His friends admired him. He was a top-flight salesman and purchasing agent for Cidema.

Frequently when a called missionary in North America makes such an adjustment in his income in order to obey the divine will, his church friends encourage him and appreciate his depth of consecration. But Miguel and his family knew their friends in El Salvador would probably take a dim view of their taking such a drastic step-down in their income. They would be criticized severely. Probably some of their closest friends, Christians and unbelievers alike, would call them crazy.

However, Miguel had promised to pray. As he and his family kept this matter before the Lord, they sensed an increasing burden for the work in Costa Rica and began to realize that God was saying, "Go!"

But even after the Mejías had decided that they would accept the challenge and walk in the new light they had received, they were forced to face a new obstacle. Miguel's boss at Cidema called him in for an interview and enthusiastically proposed a substantial raise in salary.

Up to this point, Miguel had not advised his boss about his plans for a radical change in his career. But now was the time to declare his decision. He invited his boss out to lunch the following day and carefully explained what had occurred. His boss was impressed with Miguel's openness and expressed his appreciation, but he naturally hated to lose this valuable salesman.

Of course, the family's decision to move to Costa Rica was a definite loss to the new church in El Salvador. Double tithers with good incomes— laymen who went far beyond the double tithe and invested generously in special projects for the church—were not common in the new missions that were being established by the Church of the Nazarene in El Salvador.

But El Salvador's loss was Costa Rica's gain. After all, our international church really is one. The same spirit of generosity that had characterized this family in El Salvador continued in their new assignment. Of course, they didn't have as much money to share, but they kept on double tithing. Also Enid, their younger daughter, carried her expertise in Bible quizzing, which she had developed in El Salvador, and established a similar program in Costa Rica.

Without doubt, one of the struggles the Mejías must have experienced during those days when they were seeking God's direction concerning their move was the question of the education they had hoped to make possible for their children. But if that was a struggle, the way the Lord has intervened and given those four young people an unusual exposure to educational opportunities underlines the sovereignty and providence of God.

Omar studied piano under famous teachers in London, Rome, and Paris, and even had the honor of playing the piano before the queen of England. He realized his ambition to become a world-famous pianist and later became El Salvador's ambassador for fine arts in the United States.

Aracely studied at Bethany Nazarene College (now Southern Nazarene University), at European Nazarene Bible College, and in advanced courses in Germany. Her present employment gives her opportunity to delve into scholarly projects and perfect her art in writing. Enid studied at MidAmerica Nazarene College and in Germany. And currently Miguel, Jr., is working on a master's degree at a university in Costa Rica. If Miguel and Celia struggled with temptations to reject the divine call on the basis of the negative effect their decision might have on the academic development of their children, they probably have chuckled many times over the emptiness of such fears!

Miguel and Celia gave themselves unstintingly to their new responsibilities in Costa Rica and discovered multiplied opportunities to use their expertise and to share what the Lord was giving them. They gave a used car to a fellow professor. And when they received notice that an investment Miguel had made during his days with Cidema had produced sizable profits, they did not use this for themselves. They invested it in scholarships for the students in our seminary in Costa Rica.

The international Church of the Nazarene granted them the status of associate missionaries and eventually invited them to Guatemala to become a part of the staff in the regional office for the Mexico and Central America Region. When they left Costa Rica to accept this call, they donated their home in Costa Rica to the seminary, and it is being used today for housing professors of our school there.

When they reached retirement age, they traveled extensively in Central America, visiting the churches and giving careful orientation to the local church treasurers on proper bookkeeping methods.

In recent years, they have felt the Lord was asking them to give a triple tithe instead of the double tithe they had been giving ever since their early married life. Again, their answer has been a hearty "Yes!"

One of the most notable characteristics of their ministry is the element of joy. Various times Miguel has exclaimed that the Lord has permitted him the great joy of realizing his youthful ambition of working full time in God's service. "I used to give myself to God's work during my annual two weeks of vacation, but I was tied down the rest of the year as a salesman. Now I have the privilege of working full time for the Lord." His face literally beams as he gives this testimony, and the natural enthusiasm of his voice emphasizes his sincerity.

In September 1993, I heard Miguel preach a powerful sermon on giving everything back to the Lord, since the Lord is the source of all our benefits. His concept of Christian stewardship is not simply the "health and wealth gospel." He does occasionally testify that the Lord gives more to those who give, but he clarifies this statement by assuring his listeners that the reason the Lord gives more is that he trusts His generous children to use those gifts to help others. They are not for selfish investments.

These faithful runners in the race continue to enter into new territory. May the light of their total commitment and generosity inspire fellow Christians in many countries to keep pressing forward toward perfection, as God reveals to them the contents of the "unknown bundle" they laid on the altar when God sanctified them.

5

Faithful Under Fire

WHEN BOMBS ARE EXPLODING and machine guns are spitting out death, missionaries, pastors, and lay leaders of a church face a significant decision. The alternative of escaping to a more friendly situation nags at their minds day and night. This is especially true for those who have children to protect. But the question of staying with the people who need them more than ever also burns in their conscience: "If I run for safety and leave my brothers and sisters now, what will become of them while they are under fire? Does my presence help them remain true to the Lord and grow spiritually in the midst of the conflict? Or am I a burden because they will feel obligated to take great risks in order to protect me and my family?"

Missionaries Robert and Sheila Hudson faced these alternatives in the first years of the civil war in El Salvador. When the Hudsons arrived in 1978, Nazarene missionaries who had previously served in that country had been assigned to other fields and had left eight established churches. There were also three new seminary graduates recently arrived from

Costa Rica. Their presence doubled the number of seminary-trained pastors. Rev. Hudson testifies that someone told him that he and his family had the best opportunity that planet Earth could offer a missionary! The Hudsons hit the ground running.

But within a few months promise faded into peril. Terrorist attacks turned that beautiful Central American country into a nightmare. The army fired the president. Right-wing groups accused the Roman Catholic archbishop of being a leftist and murdered him. Later, four nuns were killed. Left-wing terrorists began kidnapping wealthy businessmen and demanding multimillion-dollar ransoms. Delay spelled death.

Terrorists entered our churches and at gunpoint demanded that tithes and offerings be turned over to them. One of our members was killed when a sniper indiscriminately attacked people on a bus. The government found it necessary to enact a curfew, and buses stopped running at 7 P.M. This effectively closed the doors of our churches for night services.

It would have been easy for the Hudsons and some of our pastors to decide that their ministry would be more effective in a more auspicious atmosphere, where they would be free to carry on a full program of church activities. But the Hudsons stayed on the job until their regular furlough time, and our pastors took great risks during 10 long years of civil strife.

The Hudsons later evaluated the effects of those war years and declared that the deadly fighting in the capital city caused people to flock to evangelical churches. Robert writes, "Three years later, the Church of the Nazarene had tripled and was far beyond the goals that had seemed so high when the war began." Sheila testifies that in four short years the district grew from 400 to 1,200 persons and that they were able to organize 16 new churches and establish numerous missions and preaching points during those years.

Robert explains this growth this way: "God asked the Salvadoran Nazarenes to be a light in the midst of a dark war." He points out that in order to grow, there must be increased dependence on God and on ourselves. He declares that all-night prayer services were matched with more active participation on the part of laypersons in the weekly responsibilities of the church. In fact, with few exceptions, laypersons were the ones who started the new churches, giving the pastors greater opportunity to dedicate their efforts to the mother churches.

A person may naturally ask, "How did the constant tragedies affect the missionaries' children during those war years?" The Hudsons' daughter Kara tells her story:

> We would always go to the center of the house during battles as a precaution from stray bullets. There were no lights because the electric plant had been bombed. These were times for our family to grow closer.

> When I was eight, my sister's doctor was kidnapped. Kim and I went to school with his children. This was not an uncommon occurrence. The chil-

dren of the kidnapped person would usually continue to come to school, but no one would talk to them about it. This kidnapping was more personal to me. After what seemed like an eternity of waiting, the kidnapped doctor was released.

It doesn't require much imagination to realize the moments of terror Kim and Kara must have experienced when they would identify with their friends and consider what might happen if their own parents were kidnapped! But Kara doesn't dwell on this. She emphasizes the positive aspects of that period of her life and sees it as a time of developing her faith in God. She testifies, "I pray that I will always have the confidence of knowing that whatever the circumstance, He is with me."

Sheila also emphasizes her own spiritual growth during those years. She declares that, despite the fact they saw the dead lying on the streets almost daily and she was never sure her husband would return after he left in the morning, they had grown in their life with Christ. "It was worth every minute of struggle," she said, "because it was during those times we grew. And so did the church."

It is important to note that national pastors and laymen were just as faithful under fire as were the missionaries. Ricardo Santamaría, current pastor of our Santa Ana Church, laments that all of his children have been born in "an atmosphere of war, hate, and pain. They really are children of war."

Ricardo, his parents, and his brothers and sisters were members of our First Church in the capital city. His mother was so youthful in appearance,

The young Santamaría family. Ricardo is in the very back. Haydée is second from the right, standing.

even after having given birth to six or more children, that she looked more like their sister than their mother. In fact, she took part with them in Bible quiz practices for several weeks before the leaders discovered that she was not a teenager! No one had explained to her that the quiz program was designed for teens only. So she joyfully jumped and answered questions as capably as did her bright children.

When someone finally informed her of the age limits, she cheerfully took to the sidelines and encouraged her children to be winners. There were periods when the entire quiz team from First Church was made up of Santamarías—and they were hard to beat!

Among those young Santamarías, Ricardo especially stood out as being a highly talented public speaker. He enjoyed doing humorous readings and was a favorite for youth programs. He recited poetry that mimicked rustic peasants; he was a natural entertainer.

More important than his gifts was his keen desire to be useful in winning others to the Lord. One creative method he used was to get some of his unsaved friends together to study the Bible quiz questions with them and encourage them to become involved in the district quiz program.

Ricardo's sister Haydée (eye-DAY-ay) was also quite promising. She went to Bible college and studied for the ministry and helped conduct Vacation Bible Schools during her vacations. She later copastored a new mission with Morena Lemus, whose story will be included later in this chapter.

The Santamaría family suffered much more serious consequences of the civil war than did many other families in our church. Ricardo recounts one dreadful incident as follows:

> My heart was pounding so hard that I could barely hear what the guerrillas were saying. They were yelling at us and commanding us to lie down on the floor, facedown, with our hands behind our backs. They moved around among us and kicked us and shoved us. Then all of a sudden I heard some shots and was so frightened that for a split second I

was sure they had shot *me*. Then I realized it was someone else and turned cautiously, afraid that any movement might make me the next target. One of my brothers was slumped in a puddle of blood.

The guerrillas warned us not to move and threatened us: "Do not move, or we'll shoot all of you too. This will teach him not to support the military," the leftist guerrilla barked. To tell the truth, I could hardly breathe because of the foul odor of the gunsmoke that hung in the air as the leftists went running out the door.

But even this tragic event had its positive value. Ricardo had been somewhat open to a divine call to the ministry and probably was dimly conscious that this was his calling, but he had not really nailed it down. This narrow scrape with death awakened him to the necessity of making a complete consecration to the Lord. Soon El Salvador had another bright Nazarene studying in our seminary in Costa Rica.

For several years, Ricardo has pastored our Santa Ana Church in El Salvador. Coupled with this he has sponsored a day school in his church and has been in charge of CENETA (the Spanish acronym for Affiliated Nazarene Theological Education Centers) in his country. He has also written an unpublished book on the Salvadoran Nazarene Bible quiz program, of which he and his family were such a vital part during his teen years.

He continues as pastor in Santa Ana, now in a new relationship with his district superintendent. His sister Haydée married Guillermo Perdomo several years ago. They had a lovely wedding in the Santa Ana Church. Later they assumed the responsibility of pastoring the Chalchuapa Church. In November of 1993, the El Salvador Church of the Nazarene was divided into three districts, and Guillermo Perdomo was elected as district superintendent of the western portion of the country. Guillermo and Haydée continue to pastor the Chalchuapa Church, and Guillermo carries on his superintendent's responsibilities. The new relationship for Ricardo is interesting. His brother-in-law is now his district superintendent.

Another story of faithfulness under fire comes from Javier Jiménez (ha-vee-AIR hee-MEN-ace). Javier, who is currently pastoring our Los Santos Church of the Nazarene in San Salvador, is a graduate of our seminary in Costa Rica and has served faithfully for at least 20 years. He is another of our workers who must have met the temptation to flee to a friendlier environment. He, his wife, and four daughters have faced the fire in an encounter that easily could have taken their lives, but the angels of the Lord encamped around them while bombs and bullets threatened.

In November 1989, during one of the many skirmishes between military troops and leftist guerrillas, some of the latter took refuge in homes in the area of our Los Santos parsonage. Unfortunately, they also chose the Nazarene parsonage for cover. Javier and his family sought shelter under their table and for added protection pulled their mattresses off the beds and hid under them. While they were in this makeshift foxhole, two bombs were dropped on the parsonage, destroying a part of the roof near the room where they were huddled together.

For around seven hours, planes crisscrossed the area and strafed the innocent and the guilty. But no more bombs fell on the parsonage. However, it is easy to imagine the high tension experienced by the five ladies and the one man who felt responsible for them as they heard nearby explosions. Their prayers, expressions of their fears and eventually their praise, would make a better book than this one!

Seven hours would have seemed like an eternity of suspense, but Javier's testimony after this terrifying experience is characteristic of his Christian optimism. Instead of complaining about those seemingly everlasting hours of torture, he praises the Lord for His protection and gives Him the glory for having spared their lives. The Jiménez family continues being faithful under fire.

Another pastor who seemingly met more than his share of the "fire" was Juan Xitumul (she-too-MOOL) López, a pastor borrowed from Guatemala for helping develop the work in El Salvador. Juan is an earnest, hardworking, and successful pastor. One of his strong points is his ability to encourage his members to tithe and give generous offerings for the Lord's work. Another of his outstanding achievements can be observed in the rapid growth in membership of some of the churches he has pastored. He also served efficiently as district treasurer for several years.

Really, Guatemalans who came to serve in El Salvador were missionaries in their own right, since they had to experience culture shock in various forms. There were vocabulary differences in some cases and different expressions that were important. In Juan's case, he had been reared in a mountainous rural community and in some respects had lived a protected life. Now he found himself in a boisterous capital city, surrounded by dangers he had never encountered before.

But he tackled his job with enthusiasm. His expertise became especially evident when he helped plant our Santa Lucía Church on the outskirts of San Salvador. He and his people worked together to make their dream come true and began services in a mere shell of their new building with a bare earth floor, no windows, no bathrooms, no platform, and no electricity. They were able to hook into the electric lines of a home next door to the church because of the kindness of that neighbor, but there were occasions when someone in that house evidently forgot the importance of that connection and cut off the lights right during the night services. Juan and his people would light candles and proceed with their worship.

Our Santa Lucía Nazarenes decided to invest in a public-address system even before they installed doors and windows in the building, so it was necessary for Juan to take all that equipment back and forth from home to church during the first few months of his ministry in that church. Public-address systems, by the way, are favorite treasures for thieves in Latin America. Some of our churches have suffered sizable losses when thieves have found clever ways to break in and carry off all their sound equipment.

New Nazarenes in the Santa Lucía Church were not familiar with the traditional rules about Sabbath observance. I recall the initial shock I experienced at the close of a Sunday morning service. The pastor had barely pronounced the final "Amen" when a group of industrious members came pushing wheelbarrow loads of dirt into the sanctuary and dumping them in the area where they were beginning the construction of their platform. "Remember the Sabbath day by keeping it holy" (Exod. 20:8) apparently had a different connotation for those enthusiastic new Nazarenes! This was the one day they had free from their regular work program. It was an opportune time to work on the house of the Lord. And they took their job seriously.

The Lord blessed Juan's pastoral efforts, so that in service after service the makeshift altar was filled with earnest seekers, and consequently sizable groups became members by profession of faith.

But success does not necessarily mean freedom from problems! Right while the church was glowing and growing, Juan almost lost his wife and the new baby they were expecting. Ada was nearing the day for the delivery of their second child when a combination of high blood pressure and other complications caused her doctor to warn that she probably could not live through this pregnancy. He also predicted that the child would die before birth.

Nazarenes in El Salvador united their earnest intercession with fellow Nazarenes in Lakeland, Florida, who took the situation seriously—and the God of miracles answered. Today Eliseo, the expected (yet unexpected) unborn child, is a strapping teenager. He graduated from high school May 28, 1994. And Ada, Juan's wife, continues laboring at his side as a coworker for Christ.

But other problems, especially related to the growing political dilemma in El Salvador, began to complicate Juan's ministry. A group of leftists painted their propaganda on the wall the church had constructed around their property to protect it. Of course, this graffiti was offensive to our fellow Christians, but those who had done the painting warned Pastor Juan that if his people removed their propaganda, they would bomb the church.

Tensions increased between left and right, and one night, while Juan was returning home from the church, he was attacked by thieves, who demanded the evening offering, which he was carrying home for safety. Juan is a bold person, much more courageous than the average. Instead of delivering the offering, he told the criminals that they had no right to that money. "This is the Lord's money," he declared. They were not favorably impressed. They shot him, grabbed the money, and fled.

Juan was rushed to the hospital but was released too soon. For some reason the doctor who attended him did not discover that he still had the bullet in his body. Juan still felt completely miserable, so he returned to the hospital. This time the bullet was discovered, and the doctor let Juan know that if that bullet had moved just a small fraction of a centimeter, his body would have been paralyzed for the rest of his life.

It would be easy to assume that this was more than enough pressure on one hardworking Guatemalan who was serving in El Salvador, but this was not all. The Santa Lucía Church of the Nazarene had grown more rapidly than any of our other churches, and this fact must have inspired the opposition to overt action. Or perhaps it was the evidence that Juan was an efficient organizer that had drawn the attention of the leftist guerrillas.

One night when Juan was riding home from church on his motorcycle he was stopped by a group of leftists, who also were mounted on motorcycles. They told him in no uncertain terms that he was to become a Communist and that he was to influence all other Nazarene pastors and bring them into the Communist party. If not, they would kill him! A man who had been shot by merciless thieves knew that these men meant business. The following morning he hurried to the United States Embassy and reported the events of the previous night. Thanks to the wisdom and courtesy of those who received his report, Juan and his family were immediately whisked out of El Salvador and given residence in the United States. His new friends in Texas could not believe that he had received such prompt service from the embassy, but God works in strange, mysterious ways His wonders to perform!

Juan immediately took a pastorate in a Hispanic Nazarene church in Harlingen, Texas, and served there for several years. Later, he accepted an assignment in one of our churches in Mercedes, Texas, and continues to pastor effectively in that church today. In his six years there, Sunday School attendance has almost doubled, and in 1993 he and his members added five new Sunday School rooms to their facility.

However, he has not lost his love for El Salvador and Guatemala. He and Ada return to visit when they can afford the trip, and Juan has expressed his hope that some day the Lord will let him pastor in Central America again.

The guerrillas didn't give up on our Santa Lucía Church even after Juan and his family had been rescued and rushed out of the country. The new pastor also faced the fire of the opposition. Communist guerrillas sent word that the pastor had to deliver the equivalent of $400 at a given time or his church building would be bombed. He informed them that his church could not possibly give that amount but that they could give a portion of it. He was able to satisfy their desires with the substitute amount, and the church building still stands today.

Salvadoran Nazarenes have remained faithful during the intense fires of the 10-year war. May they keep on running and illuminating others with holy fire, that of divine truth!

6

Other Faithful Runners

MARCELINO TZÍN (TSEEN) became God's choice for pastoring First Church in San Salvador after a failed coup attempt for that pastorate. An overambitious young man had campaigned before the annual meeting and felt assured of his own election, but the Lord stepped into the sticky situation and worked through unanticipated channels to achieve victory for His cause. (The politically motivated candidate eventually was declared persona non grata by the Salvadoran government because it was discovered that he was bringing Guatemalan produce across the border without a license. He was barred from returning to El Salvador.)

Marcelino loved his people into a healthy fellowship. He and his wife found ready acceptance even with the group that had been temporarily duped by the organized campaign for power on the part of the above-mentioned party.

There are some interesting firsts attached to Marcelino's name. The most obvious, of course, is the fact that he was pastor of *First* Church. He was also our first Nazarene pastor in El Salvador who bought a car. The pastors themselves voted for this use of funds that had been provided by a special offering from some of our churches in the United States. They knew the funds were limited, so they generously voted to give this privilege to Marcelino Tzín and to Juan Xitumul López. They felt that these two needed this advantage more than the other pastors on the district.

Marcelino had studied for the ministry and was a good Bible preacher and an unusually capable pastor, but driving a car had not been a part of his preparation for the pastorate. He had to be a pretty brave soul to enter the rushing traffic of that capital city as a complete novice behind the wheel!

Marcelino was also our first pastor who had a baptistery in his church. Up to that point, all Nazarene baptisms had taken place in the beautiful Lake Ilopango—or, in one exceptional case, in a rather muddy stream. It was a historic day when Marcelino initiated that baptistery in First Church. When the children found out about the service, they asked permission to stay in the adult service instead of having their junior church service. Of course, baptisms are an emotion-filled event in almost any church, but in that first baptismal service at First Church, God's presence was very real, and the congregation was especially blessed. One of the most precious aspects of that service was the wide-eyed response of the group of children who crowded around the baptistery as close as possible and eagerly watched every detail. They would never forget that moving experience.

Marcelino was also the first non-North American who served as district superintendent in El Salvador. The Lord used him to set the pace for the very young Salvadoran who would follow him, but he experienced the same call back home that several other Guatemalans had confronted. Guatemalan Nazarenes needed him.

Today Marcelino is the district superintendent of our Petén District in Guatemala. That assignment is quite different from the one he fulfilled in El Salvador. His work takes him in a small canoe across the huge and deep Lake Petén to preach in our Flores Church, located on an island in the lake. It also takes him across the lake to churches located on the opposite shore or through the jungle to a river on the other side, one still inhabited by crocodiles. He continues to be faithful in his race as he ministers in our various churches located along lakes and rivers in Petén.

Another outstanding person in our church during those formative years of Nazarene work in El Salvador was Morena Lemus. She began quite early in her youth to carry her torch for Christ. She was already a Christian when she and other members of her family began to attend our Vista Hermosa Church of the Nazarene in San Salvador.

Morena was one among nine children in the Lemus family. She, her mother, and her sisters all had the perfect teeth that contribute to the "million-dollar smile." And the Lemus girls had the added advantage of having lovely long hair. Theirs was an attractive family.

Morena was the type of person a Sunday School teacher enjoys having in a youth class. She showed keen interest in the truths being presented and gave evidence of spiritual growth as she put into practice the truths she was discovering. She was also eager to take part in public services. As soon as the Bible quiz program was inaugurated, she and three of her sisters became team members, and they studied consistently and piled up many winning points for the Vista Hermosa Church.

Morena recognized a divine call to the ministry quite early and went with other young Salvadorans to our Bible college in Guatemala. When she returned, she joined with Haydée Santamaría and helped open a new mission. Both girls were at risk in that area of the capital but worked faithfully at their task. Later, Morena saw her need for advanced studies and enrolled in our seminary in Costa Rica. But in the meantime, a significant change occurred in her life—a change that affected many other Salvadoran Nazarenes as well.

The Holy Spirit had been working in several of our Salvadoran pastors and leaders, creating within them an increasing appetite for more knowledge concerning the doctrine of entire sanctification. By 1974, this hunger had reached the point that they asked for special holiness classes. These classes were arranged on the basis of their receiving credit in our seminary in Costa Rica. The rector there, Rev. Howard Conrad, helped implement this plan, and classes were begun once a week in the Jardín Church in the capital.

There was excellent attendance and lively participation in those classes. Pastors and other workers from Santa Ana, San Miguel, and the churches in the capital came together to discuss carefully the contents of six holiness books, five of which had been translated into Spanish. The total course covered about 90 hours of class.

As we missionaries listened to class debates and student reflections, one often-repeated theme concerned us. Almost every student in the group thought of holiness as keeping a rigid set of rules. Sometimes they sounded like dogmatic Pharisees. This concern deepened as nearly a third of the course had passed and the students were still holding firmly to their legalistic interpretation of entire sanctification.

Morena Lemus was a member of this class. For the session scheduled for November 5, 1974, she had been asked to make an oral report on 50 pages from one of the textbooks. As was her custom, she studied her assignment thoroughly. As she studied, the Holy Spirit quickened her understanding so that she began to realize that entire sanctification was much more than rule-keeping. Her heart longed for something she had never experienced before—an experience of divine grace that would help her love and forgive those who mistreated her, an experience of divine love in her heart that would give her victory over her jealousy, her pride, and her selfishness. She faced the fact that her Christian life definitely did not measure up to what she was discovering in the textbook.

Before class started that special November morning, she came to the teacher and tearfully confessed that she really was not capable of presenting the material she had studied. God was dealing with her heart in such a way that she knew she would break down and have to confess her need to the entire group. But as she and the teacher talked it over, she came to the conclusion that this was exactly the right thing to do.

After the opening prayer, she walked resolutely before the class and gave her confessional testimony, then turned and dropped down at the altar and began to ask the Lord to come into her heart and sanctify her.

This was God's time. For a long time He had been preparing the class members for this special moment. He would have poured out His Spirit on them long before that eventful day, but apparently class members had felt more comfortable discussing peripheral issues than they felt in facing heart matters. Now, one by one, other members of the class added their own confessions and joined Morena at the altar.

That wonderful morning a holiness revival broke out among our leaders. God had used the honest confession of one sincere young lady to help break down the resistance that had been maintained for all those weeks. His Spirit came upon that class in sanctifying power, and the class was never the same again. What a difference there was in class discussions after that eventful morning!

Of course, the revival didn't stop with the pastors and lay leaders who were participating in that holiness class. The revival extended into our churches as class members shared their vibrant testimonies with fellow Christians and invited them to come and experience for themselves what Christ had died to make possible for them—a wholly sanctified life.

Morena felt led to continue her studies and eventually graduated from our seminary in Costa Rica. During her years there, she fell in love with Ascensio de Santa Cruz, a fellow student from Peru, and they married and accepted a pastorate in our Moravia Church in San José, Costa Rica. The Lord gave them two lively little boys, Esdras and Ezer.

In 1992 they moved to a pastorate in El Bosque (BOSE-kay), another section of San José. This new assignment is especially difficult, since a Satanist group is located in that area. Because of this challenge, Morena has developed a special ministry of prayer and frequently deals directly with demon-possessed neighbors. Her years of memorizing portions of the Bible for Bible quizzes have provided special strength during those tense moments when she is dealing with these tragic cases. At least three different persons have threatened to kill her as she was dealing with the demons to whom they had dedicated their lives. But the Lord has given her tremendous faith and a sense of boldness in the presence of these threats. Life in the Spirit has prepared her to carry her torch high and far.

In the same Sunday School class and on the same Bible quiz team in which Morena and her sisters participated were two engaging brothers, Oscar and Jaime (HIGH-may) Villanueva. Jaime was the more mischievous of the two, but both were full of good humor and helped make youth activities in their church attractive to other young people.

If Oscar were given an opportunity to tell his story, he would flash a broad smile and begin by saying that the Lord had beautifully saved him during his early teen years but that while the missionaries were on furlough, he had slipped back into sin and had gone deeper into evil than he had before his conversion:

> When the missionaries returned from their furlough, I was absolutely miserable. I recall that one evening I was standing in front of the house that was being rented for services in Vista Hermosa and was trying to make up my mind as to whether I would go inside. I was depressed and was looking down at my shoes when Mrs. Bryant walked up and started talking to me. She invited me into the church service, and I didn't realize till she confessed to me later that I had changed so much that she didn't even recognize me at first. Sin had left its marks on me more than I knew. That bothered me.
>
> I didn't repent immediately, but the Lord dealt gently and firmly with me till I finally made up my mind that I wanted more out of life than the so-called pleasures of the world. I was so hungry for salvation that I went to the altar and sought earnestly till I found deep peace. This time I decided that I never would go back into sin again. I recall having testified in one of our services that "no one who puts his hand to the plow and looks back is fit

for service in the kingdom of God" (Luke 9:62). I applied that verse to my own life and determined to be faithful.

This time Oscar went on and was sanctified. He had to make some important ethical decisions as he entered new phases of his walk with Christ. He had graduated from high school at the top of his class, having specialized in accounting and taken a job in an office.

Not too long afterward, he began to receive phone calls and telegrams from a competing company that evidently had knowledge of his high grades in school and wanted a man of that ability as an accountant. They offered him a much higher salary than the one he was currently receiving. Oscar talked this over with one of the missionaries and explained why he was determined not to accept that tempting offer. The competing company handled some products that were quite acceptable, but they also sold liquor, and he felt that since liquor had been one of his own problems, he couldn't invest his time and efforts in a company that sold liquor to others.

It is interesting to note that Oscar was not very familiar with the *Manual of the Church of the Nazarene*. He was not basing his decision on church rules. His conscience and the guidance of the Holy Spirit were the basis of his refusal to take the job that offered higher pay.

Some of his peers pressured him mercilessly and accused him of not being fair to his mother and sister, who would profit greatly from his increased salary. One woman even phoned one of the missionaries and tried to get support for her contention that he should take the new job. Of course, the missionary asked the friend if she wanted Oscar to go back into his old life of sin. The friend said, "No, but his family needs that money!"

Oscar stood firmly by his decision. A few months later, the missionary asked him about how he was coming along in his employment. He gladly announced that he was then receiving from the original employer *exactly* the same amount that the competing company had offered him! Obviously, God doesn't always shower His blessings that immediately, but in His time His "payday" arrives.

However, the Lord wanted more than Oscar's willingness to apply his Christian ethics to that job situation in the office. God had His own office job for him. As a much-involved layman, Oscar began to see the need to lend his services as a pastor. He hadn't recognized a divine call to the ministry, so he continued his work at the office and pastored our Jardín Church. But as the months passed, the members of that church recognized Oscar's possibilities and asked him to go to Costa Rica to obtain formal academic preparation for the pastorate. They told him they would pay his tuition and other expenses. Their only requirement was that he pastor *their* church when he graduated.

They kept their word, and Oscar kept his. Now for several years he has effectively pastored the Jardín Church of the Nazarene in San Salvador. It is growing and may eventually need to move to a place where adequate parking space and Sunday School rooms can be provided.

Oscar's brother, Jaime, who also became a Nazarene in Vista Hermosa Church, is still studying at Nazarene University in Costa Rica. He is working on his master's degree and is pastoring for a sister denomination. He has around 700 members in his congregation.

These Villanueva boys, who began their Christian race in our Vista Hermosa Church, were strongly influenced by a self-sacrificing lady pastor, a Salvadoran who had graduated at the top of her class in Costa Rica. She was at that time María Julia Martínez. She and her husband, Ramón Campos, deserve a chapter all their own.

Trophies of Grace

M ARÍA JULIA, WHAT IS THE MEANING of all those trophies you have on that shelf?"

María Julia looked confused. "What do you mean? I've never won a trophy in all my life."

She followed the eyes of the interviewer and wrinkled her forehead. Her own eyes expressed curiosity. "You *did* win first place in your class when you graduated from the Nazarene seminary in Costa Rica, didn't you?" her interviewer asked.

"Yes," she replied, "but I didn't receive any trophies for that."

"OK! I may seem to be playing with words, but I'm thinking seriously about the many new Nazarenes whose lives you have influenced across the years. The Lord has used you to make an indelible impression on Oscar and Jaime Villanueva, on the whole Lemus family—especially on their girls: Morena, Alba Fe, Salma, and Coralia. You became family to some who had left a Roman Catholic church and who felt uncomfortable with their close relatives who had not made this change. The Lord only knows how many trophies of grace stand on that invisible shelf behind you. I'd say you have a mighty good track record."

"Well, if that's what you mean, I myself am a trophy of grace. God's prevenient grace reached me while I was a sinner living in San Francisco, California. He saved me, but really I didn't become an actively involved Christian till after I had returned from there to my home in Santa Ana, El Salvador."

"Tell me how you became a Nazarene."

"God used an interesting contact to help me make that decision. An elderly lady who belonged to the Lutheran Church was occasionally attending the Church of the Nazarene and kept urging me to visit that church. I don't think she ever became a Nazarene herself, but it was through her insistence that I decided to attend. I liked the people and their message, so I eventually joined the church. It was during those months in that church that the Lord called me to the ministry. It was a definite call, so definite that I would have sinned if I had failed to obey the divine mandate."

After the trouble at our Vista Hermosa Church, it seemed wise to change pastors and to give Rafael Flores and his family a different pastorate. The fresh start was wholesome for them. Since María Julia Martínez had recently graduated from seminary, she was available for filling the vacancy at the Vista Hermosa Church.

It is highly probable that María Julia had not pictured herself as a specialist in youth ministries, but the young people liked her and flocked to the church. She was willing to stay after services to counsel and pray with them about their personal problems.

Her mother had given her a refrigerator, and María was quite generous in sharing whatever food she might have stored in that pastoral accessory. She maintained an open door, an open Bible, an open pocketbook, an open refrigerator, and an open heart. And, as mentioned previously, the trouble-makers didn't feel at home there. They went else-where, and the church in Vista Hermosa flourished as the Lord brought revival to His people and new converts joined the church.

María Julia joined enthusiastically in the district youth program and took active part in preparing her own young people, as well as those from other Nazarene churches, for Bible quiz tournaments. She was full of energy and was willing to work long, extra hours to see the church grow.

During her years of study in Costa Rica, María Julia had become acquainted with a handsome young Salvadoran named Ramón Campos. He was a fellow student, but neither paid much attention to the other. They maintained a rather casual friendship, but nothing that even approached a romance.

Ramón Campos and his parents had attended church services in a Holiness denomination during the years that they lived in Honduras, but when they moved to San Miguel, El Salvador, there were no churches of that denomination in the city. However, their new home was located near the Church of the Nazarene.

At that time Stanley and Norma Storey were

pastoring the San Miguel congregation. When the Campos family visited the Church of the Nazarene, Stanley and Norma joyfully reached out to them and made them feel welcome. Ramón was nourished under the friendly pastoral care of these two missionaries until the day he moved to Costa Rica to start his own preparation for ministry.

Unfortunately, during his years in the seminary, Ramón identified with a small but influential group of students who were opposed to the doctrine of Holiness. They would make fun of other students who had taken the doctrine seriously. To make matters worse, Ramón had a strong temper and found it difficult to control. Sanctification would have made a notable difference in his Christian life, but he belonged to the rejecters and maintained his loyalty to them.

When he finished his studies in the seminary and returned to El Salvador, my husband, Larry, asked him to serve as pastor in our Jardín Church in the capital city. He took his new assignment quite seriously, and we had no idea that he was struggling with a difficult-to-manage temper and had identified with the opposition regarding the doctrine of entire sanctification. But the Lord knew and certainly was dealing with him concerning his spiritual needs.

As Ramón dealt with others, the Lord talked to him about his own needs, and he began to work at the job of controlling his anger. While he was struggling in this area of his Christian life, he met some really tough tests. One of these occurred one Saturday when he was returning from having preached at one of the new missions located several kilometers from the capital.

Ramón was seated comfortably on a full bus and was concentrating on the material in his Sunday School quarterly, since he was scheduled to teach an adult class the following day. Suddenly, he became conscious of the fact that in the aisle an intoxicated man was taking improper liberties with an attractive young lady. Ramón thought fast and quickly stood and offered the girl his seat. He then stood in front of her and gave her protection from the abusive aggressor.

It took the offender a few seconds to realize what had happened. By that time, Ramón, though standing, was concentrating again on the Sunday School lesson in his quarterly. The other man became furious and challenged Ramón to a fight. He made an ugly scene, but Ramón kept on reading his lesson. He decided to try to ignore the fellow. Finally, the intoxicated fellow knocked Ramón's glasses onto the floor of the bus, broke them, then knocked Ramón down. Momentarily, Ramón blacked out.

Not everyone on that bus was a Christian valiantly fighting with his own anger and trying to overcome his own nasty temper. In fact, it is highly possible that Ramón was the only born-again Christian on that full bus. So his fellow passengers took the matter in hand and roughly shoved the intruder out the front door of the bus and let him walk off his drunken rage.

Ramón was perfectly capable of protecting

himself. He was a muscular young man and definitely not a "wimp," but there was more at stake. He testified later that he had made up his mind that he was not going to let that unruly fellow passenger rob him of the victories he had begun to win in his walk with Christ.

This was a great victory, but the Lord had much more grace to offer to Ramón Campos. He was one of those hungry-hearted pastors who knelt at the altar in our Jardín Church on that eventful day in November 1974 when the Lord had begun a Holiness revival with the confession of Morena Lemus. He has been a remarkably changed man ever since.

Both Ramón Campos and María Julia Martínez were popular and could have had their choice among various possibilities for a romance. There certainly were interested candidates, but little by little they began to notice each other. A storybook romance developed, and it eventually became evident that either the Jardín Church or the Vista Hermosa Church was going to lose a pastor, for the two pastors obviously were going to become one.

The couple asked Larry to perform the wedding ceremony in the Jardín Church, and María Julia's whole youth class from the Vista Hermosa Church served as bridesmaids and groom's attendants. What an attractive group of young people surrounded them at the altar that night as they made their solemn vows!

At least temporarily, Vista Hermosa Church was the winner, for the couple served that church as

María Julia Martínez and Ramón Campos on their wedding day.

pastors, but the time came when the Jardín Church received its turn, since Ramón and María combined their district ministry with pastoral assignments.

In 1976 Ramón was elected as the district superintendent of El Salvador. He has served in that capacity ever since and continues as superintendent of the central area now that El Salvador has been divided into three districts. He and María Julia have worked as temporary pastors in one church after another because of a shortage of pastors. In 1994, Ramón was serving as pastor of First Church in the capital, and his wife was teaching a youth class at Vista Hermosa Church.

Their two older children, Maribel and Juan Ramón, are teenagers and are actively involved in the work of the church. Maribel has made a total commitment of her life to the Lord and is quite willing to be involved in Christian service. Since she has received no definite call to the ministry, she is preparing to become an electrical engineer. Juan Ramón is still in high school but enjoys working with teams from our Nazarene colleges and universities that are involved in projects for our church in various parts of El Salvador. David, their youngest, is a joyful youngster who makes life interesting for his big brother and sister.

While one of those teams from MidAmerica Nazarene College was working in El Salvador in March 1994, Ramón's brother's wife died in childbirth, and Ramón and María Julia took on the responsibility of caring for the new baby. This means that the district parsonage rings nightly with phone calls and baby cries. One can only hope that this child will become another precious trophy of grace when she reaches her time of decision.

God's amazing grace has been evident in Ramón and María Julia during the long period of civil war that plagued their country during the greater part of their ministry. Ramón was quite young when he became district superintendent. Just assuming the normal responsibilities of his new position would have been a challenge, but there were added complications.

The increasing tensions and horrors of war, including kidnapping, guerrilla demands for money in the middle of church services, the death of fellow Nazarenes and the need to comfort heartbroken families, the curfew that made night services impossible, the threats and bombings—all these things were hard enough on the laymen and pastors, but the very young superintendent and his wife carried an even greater load.

In the midst of these traumatic situations, Ramón developed a rare physical handicap called Meige' Syndrome. It caused his eyelids to drop shut involuntarily, so that he was at risk when he was driving his car. His eyes could shut without giving any previous warning, and he couldn't open them. Of course, this condition affected his preaching also. He finally resorted to asking Maribel, his daughter, to read the Scripture portions to the congregation and often had her drive the car for him, especially if María Julia needed to be helping in a different church.

Yet even in the midst of their troubles, Ramón and his wife have grown in grace and, with God's help, still win new trophies of grace.

CAUSE and Call

TEN ORIENTATION SESSIONS are now history. The classic struggle with permits, purchasing, packaging, and packing is over. New recruits are arriving. They have their passports and visas in hand. They have just gone through customs—a harrowing episode for the inexperienced and a huge responsibility for Dr. Frank Moore and his wife, who are in charge of the 26-member CAUSE (College And University students Sharing Experiences) team.

Every student is loaded to the gills with suitcases and duffel bags. They heave a sigh of relief as they walk out the front door of the air terminal. An enthusiastic youth exclaims:

"Hey, guys! We're here! Anybody wish he could go back to Kansas?"

Someone in the crowd responds: "To Kansas and final exams? No way! I vote to stay all summer and build clinics and churches. Putting up cement block walls should be a lot more fun than memorizing the contents of 20 textbooks. By the way, I'm hungry. Does anyone have a candy bar he could share with a starving classmate?"

MidAmerica Nazarene College was the first of nine Nazarene colleges and universities that participated in CAUSE ministries in El Salvador between March 19 and June 24, 1994.

Sixteen long years passed in which no Work and Witness teams were permitted to enter El Salvador, but now the ban is lifted, and all eight of the Nazarene colleges and universities in the United States, plus Canadian Nazarene College, joyfully responded to specific needs in this Central American country.

Those suitcases and duffel bags the students carried were stuffed with clothing purchased at Wal-Mart at tremendously reduced prices. The MANC team was able to obtain clothing valued between $12,000 and $15,000. These articles of clothing were distributed among needy families—not haphazardly, but under the watchful eyes of Salvadoran Christians who are experienced in this type of ministry.

One method they used for maintaining order and avoiding confusion was to charge children 75 cents to get into the door of the distribution room, where they were allowed to "buy" three whole outfits for 25 cents apiece. Only five children were permitted to enter at one time.

With big expressive eyes dancing with anticipation, these youngsters tried on the new outfits and selected what fit their size and tastes. Along with their new clothing, each was given vitamins, iron tablets, soap, and a toothbrush. The children emerged with broad smiles of gratitude and excitement, leaving room for five new purchasers to enter. Of course, they stopped to show off their new merchandise with pride and to give experienced advice to friends who were patiently(?) waiting in line.

Most of the college students worked at the side of volunteers from our Salvadoran churches and were busily engaged in helping to construct the new "Community Health Center." A few were specialized in nurses' training, and these dedicated their time to examining children and, under the advice of the experts, to helping the children receive appropriate medicines for their needs. Many of these children had never had a medical exam before. To address the many needs of those children, the Heart to Heart organization provided $7,000 worth of medicine, and concerned members of the Church of the Nazarene donated $800 worth of vitamins and iron tablets.

Puppet ministries in the public schools in the area where the Community Health Center was being constructed opened another door for Christian service. Through puppets, the college students gave their personal testimonies and told Bible stories to the children.

If a person can imagine this scene multiplied by nine, one has a fair idea of the extensive ministry of the CAUSE teams in El Salvador in 1994. In the words of Prof. Frank Moore, the students "hit the ground running."

Behind all this involvement in Compassionate Ministries are Salvadoran evangelicals who have paved the way, opened doors, and worked around the clock to make CAUSE ministry possible. The organization called OPRODE (the Spanish acronym for Professsional Organization of Development) is a part of this picture. It consists of representatives from four different religious denominations, including the Church of the Nazarene. Members of this group are working together to serve people who have lost their homes and their employment, either as a result of the 1986 earthquake or as a consequence of the 10-year civil war.

One of the hardest working members of this group is Dr. Cecilia Meléndez, a member of our Jardín Church of the Nazarene. She has her own medical clinic in connection with her home, but she spends a great deal of her time serving in areas of the capital where the greatest needs exist. Ceci, as she is lovingly called by fellow workers, literally wears herself out trying to stretch her time and energies to meet the constant demands of those who recognize her expertise and rely on her help. She is highly trained and is quite sensitive to the divine call. In her personal devotions she keeps asking the Lord to give her specific directions for her ministry.

Dr. Meléndez was saved and came into the Church of the Nazarene under the ministry of Oscar Villanueva. She was also nurtured by missionaries Bob and Sheila Hudson. In 1993 the General Assembly elected her to serve on the General Board for the Church of the Nazarene.

There are many others who are involved in meeting the many needs of El Salvador. Rev. Carlos Ayala and his architect wife, Mayra, are pastors of the Madre Tierra congregation. This couple has been deeply involved in Compassionate Ministries ever since the terrifying earthquake of October 1986.

Right after the quake, the Ayalas organized their teenagers into a Salvadoran Work and Witness team. In an incredibly short time, these young people had put in footings and assembled metal frame structures for several homes for the destitute. The Ayalas, pastor Miguel Angel Pleitez (play-TACE), Dr. Meléndez, and other Salvadoran Nazarenes became increasingly involved in providing low-cost homes for victims of the earthquake.

Due to the efforts of these people and others like them, the Church of the Nazarene received a letter of appreciation from the Salvadoran government, recognizing our church as the first international organization that had provided this type of assistance following the earthquake. In fact, on the basis of continued involvement by our general church, the Salvadoran government asked for our help and has evaluated our housing projects as the best use of relief funds they have ever seen. The Lord is helping our church to minister to body and soul in disaster areas around the capital city with housing, clinics, and brand-new churches.

As a general church, we have a cause and a call in El Salvador. In a country ravaged by war and hatred, as well as by destructive earthquakes, the causes are evident, and the call is imperative. Work and Witness teams and CAUSE projects are highly important. But the church needs to go beyond building churches and clinics. Especially urgent is the demand for love on its knees to sustain these men and women who are struggling with anger and bitterness toward those who killed members of their families during those 10 years of civil strife. The ability to forgive is superhuman and can occur only as the love of God is poured into their hearts by the Holy Spirit. Fervent prayer by those who care can help bring a great holiness revival to churches in El Salvador.

Salvadoran Nazarenes have their own call to witness through their testimonies and through a Christlike life. And they are responding to this call. They are not satisfied with the status quo. Thirty churches are not enough. Several of them are thinking in terms of 300 Nazarene churches by the year 2010. This means a divine call to those who are to pastor that many churches. And it also involves adequate training for men and women who respond positively to the call.

Right now, District Superintendent Ramón Campos and others are offering CENETA courses to prepare their present pastors and to train others for future assignments. Our Nazarene University in Costa Rica offers a rich curriculum for those who desire to receive a master's degree in theological studies. The harvest is plenteous and the laborers are few. Pray ye therefore the Lord of the harvest that he will engrave in the hearts of His chosen reapers a burning conviction for the cause and the call.

As fellow runners in the Christian race, the total commitment on the part of people like Miguel and Celia Mejía, Ricardo Santamaría, Juan Xitumul López, Morena Lemus, Marcelino Tzín, Oscar Villanueva, María Julia Martínez de Campos, Ramón Campos, Javier Jiménez, Cecilia Meléndez, the Ayalas and Pleitez family, Stanley and Norma Storey, Bob and Sheila Hudson ("and what shall I more say of . . .") call us to action.

"Therefore, since we are surrounded by such a great cloud of witnesses, let us throw off everything that hinders and the sin that so easily entangles, and let us run with perseverance the race marked out for us. Let us fix our eyes on Jesus, the author and perfecter of our faith" (Heb. 12:1-2).